Now You See Them Now You Don't

Poems About Creatures That Hide

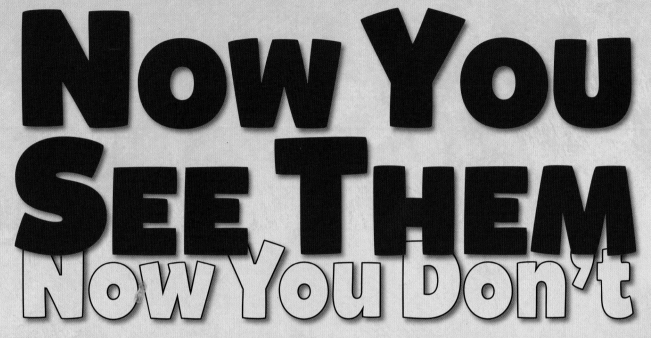

David L. Harrison

Illustrated by **Giles Laroche**

Charlesbridge

To Beth Kennon and Leslie Johnson with love
—D. L. H.
To Elliott, Emily, Leah, Pierce, and Priscilla
—G. L.

Text copyright © 2016 by David L. Harrison
Illustrations copyright © 2016 by Giles Laroche

Published by Charlesbridge
85 Main Street, Watertown, MA 02472
(617) 926-0329 • www.charlesbridge.com

Library of Congress Cataloging-in-Publication Data
Harrison, David L., author.
   Now you see them, now you don't: poems about creatures that
hide/David L. Harrison; illustrated by Giles Laroche.
      pages cm
   ISBN 978-1-58089-610-8 (reinforced for library use)
   ISBN 978-1-60734-842-9 (ebook)
   ISBN 978-1-60734-843-6 (ebook pdf)
   1. Camouflage (Biology)—Juvenile literature. 2. Protective coloration
(Biology)—Juvenile literature. 3. Adaptation (Biology)—Juvenile literature.
I. Laroche, Giles, illustrator. II. Title.
QL767.H37 2016
591.47'2—dc23   2014049184

Printed in China
(hc) 10 9 8 7 6 5 4 3 2 1

Illustrations done in cut-paper relief on a variety of hand-painted papers
Display type set in Mikado by Hannes Von Doehren
Text type set in Triplex by Emigre Graphics
Color separations by Colourscan Print Co Pte Ltd, Singapore
Printed by Imago in China
Production supervision by Brian G. Walker
Designed by Whitney Leader-Picone

CREATURES THAT HIDE

An octopus changes color and shape. A flounder blends into the ocean floor. A baby deer hides in plain sight. A copperhead coiled in autumn leaves practically disappears. A polar bear looks white like snow and ice. A walking stick looks like, well, a stick.

No matter the type of animal—sea creature, reptile, amphibian, mammal, insect, or bird—camouflage is useful. Whether an animal is the hunter or the hunted—or both—it pays to be hard to find. Turn the page to meet some animals that know how to hide . . . and see how they do it!

Sea Life

Ghost Crab

List of words
ghost crabs know:
danger, freeze,
blend, slow,
look, run,
stop, go.

Sea, food,
wave, tide,
eat, fast,
scurry, hide,
dig, hole,
dive, inside.

Gull, danger,
sand, white,
disappear,
plain, sight,
sun, burn,
safe, night.

Common Octopus

The octopus is slyly shy.
It's hard to spot it lurking by—
red or brown or murky gray
help it hide or slide away.

But slyly shy it might glide back,
slipping through the slightest crack,
and with its octo-lethal charms,
hug its prey in suckery arms.

Flounder

Like brilliant stars overhead,
schools of fish ebb and flow.
They swim above my sandy bed,
never notice me below.

Patiently I watch and wait
for fish, crabs, unwary krill
to meet me for a dinner date.
Until they're close, I lie still.

Then with sudden toothy grin,
I open wide and take them in.

Reef Stonefish

Spines of death
down its back,
it waits . . .
waits . . .
waits . . .
attack!

Rock?
Coral?

Stone still,
it waits . . .
waits . . .
waits . . .
kill.

REPTILES & AMPHIBIANS

Gray Tree Frog

Sun settles,
shadows creep,
a piping voice
begins to peep.
Deep within
its tree retreat,
it climbs and clings
with sticky feet.

Bold singer
seldom seen,
it matches forest
gray or green.
It disappears
so hungry bird
cannot find
what it just heard.

Copperhead

Dear Mr. Vole:

Find me
if you can,
my sssskin
deceivessss,
helpssss me
dissssappear
among thessse
leavessss.

Find me
if you can,
on dappled
sssstonessss,
lounging by
thissss pile of
tiny
bonessss.

Find me
if you can,
atop thissss
ledge,
a broken sssstick,
a branch
along thissss
edge.

Find me
if you can,
for if you
don't,
I'll be here
tomorrow . . .
you
won't.

Ssssincerely,
Mr. Copperhead

Young Bullfrog

Could be a clump
of rotting leaves,
a mossy,
wet-slick stone,
perched at water's edge,
alone.

Sudden croak,
leap,
splash—
gone.

Still-hungry heron,
stilt-legs on.

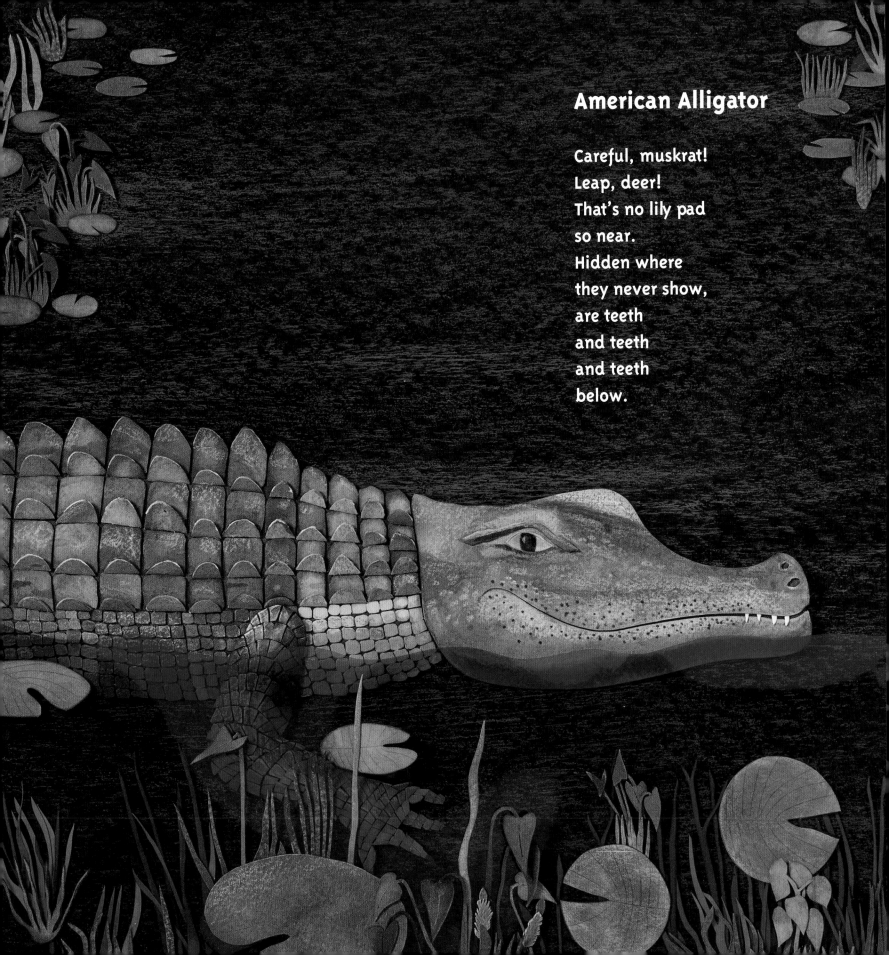

American Alligator

Careful, muskrat!
Leap, deer!
That's no lily pad
so near.
Hidden where
they never show,
are teeth
and teeth
and teeth
below.

MAMMALS

Bengal Tiger

Dappled shadows,
waving grasses,
where the gliding
hunter passes.

Pupils widen,
muscles ready,
crouches lower,
patient, steady.

Deer grazing,
crickets singing,
striped lightning,
tiger springing!

Fawn

When danger lurks,
too small to fight,
it lies down
in plain sight.
Without a scent,
the slightest trace,
to give away
its hiding place.
It's saved by fawny
polka dots
that blend with
gentle sunny spots.

Eastern Gray Squirrel

Up a tree
like a shot.
Disappears
lickety-split.
Hugs limb.
Still as bark.
Magic act—
no finding it.

Polar Bear

Seal, be wary
of the bear.
It's white on white
against the glare
when snow sparkles
the frosty air.

Seal, be watchful,
have a care.
Beside the hole,
it's waiting there.
Dive! Escape
the great white bear!

INSECTS & SPIDERS

Bumblebee Moth

A moth that looks
like a bumblebee
is nature's gimmick
to scare away
its enemies
and save the mimic.

Crab Spider

Spider used
a bloom to hide it
until a fly
flew down beside it.
Then with spider's
aptitude
the buzzy fly
became fast food.

Praying Mantis

If I could roar
like a dinosaur,
I wouldn't have to
hang on plants.
I would stomp
on pesky ants.

If I could run
like a dinosaur,
I wouldn't have to
sit so still.
I'd lunge and leap
to get my fill.

But I can't roar
like a dinosaur,
cannot gallop
after prey.
I have to wait
if it takes all day.

Walking Stick

My walk
is slow,
for
otherwise
a bird
might
see me
on this
tree
and swoop
to make
a meal
of me.
So
slow
to go
is my
disguise.
I'm never
quick,
a clever
trick,
so birds
think I'm
a tasteless
stick.

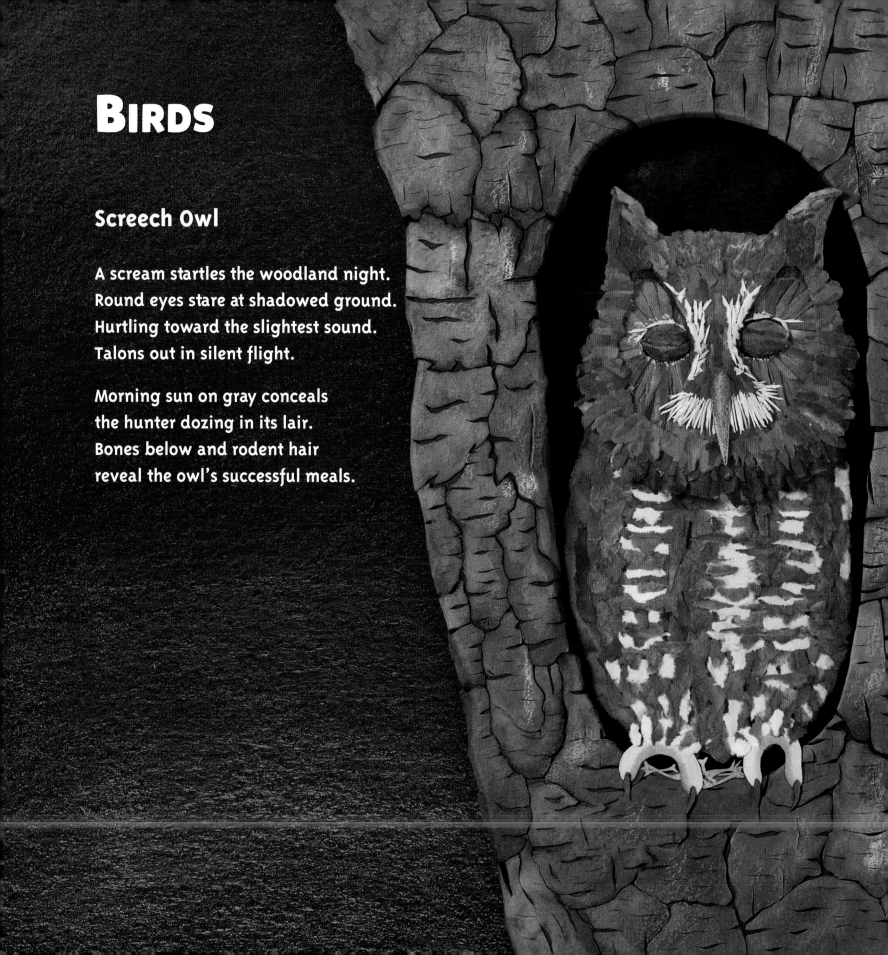

BIRDS

Screech Owl

A scream startles the woodland night.
Round eyes stare at shadowed ground.
Hurtling toward the slightest sound.
Talons out in silent flight.

Morning sun on gray conceals
the hunter dozing in its lair.
Bones below and rodent hair
reveal the owl's successful meals.

Great Blue Heron

Standing
statue
still.

Slender
sharp
bill.

Slowly
    aimed
spear.

Watching
    drawing
near.

Tasty
    treat
        observed.

Strike!
Dinner's
served.

Hawk

Look up, mouse.
See the sky?
See that tiny
speck on high?

No time to lose.
Scamper, mouse,
hide inside
your tunnel house.

Scurry, mouse,
if you are wise.
That speck you see
has hunter's eyes.

Beak that tears,
claws that hold,
dive-bombing
wings that fold.

Hurry, mouse,
avoid the shock
when the tiny speck
is suddenly hawk!

Sea Life

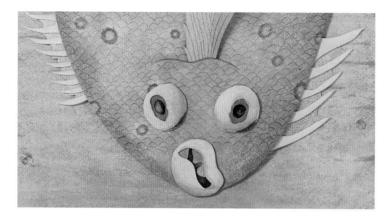

Ghost Crab *Ocypode ceratophthalmus*

The ghost crab's tunnel home can be up to four feet deep, and the beach is its roof. Ghost crabs may pop out for a quick look around, but they don't stir much by day. When they do, they blend into the sand. Night is a different story. After the birds that prey on them go to bed, ghost crabs creep out and set to work. They look like a merry band dancing in the moonlight as they feed on tiny bits of plants and animals that the waves toss onto the beach.

Common Octopus *Octopus vulgaris*

An octopus has lots of ways to defend itself: It can squirt an inky cloud and swim off. Or change color to blend with its surroundings. Or change shape to look like a bumpy rock. Or sneak across the sandy sea bottom. Because it doesn't have a skeleton, this intelligent creature can slip through cracks and fit into tight holes. A parrot-like beak allows it to tear into fish, crabs, and shrimp. Most octopuses are small, but some weigh hundreds of pounds and can even kill sharks. All species of octopuses have venom.

Flounder *Paralichthys*

When a baby flounder hatches, it has one eye on each side of its head. But as it grows older, one eye slowly moves until both are on the same side. Adult flounders have flat bodies and live on the ocean floor. They change color to blend in with the sand. Flounders thrive in shallow water but can survive in the deepest ocean trenches. Flounders are aggressive hunters: when a fish, shrimp, or crab wanders too close, what looks like an innocent patch of sand erupts and lashes out with incredible speed.

Reef Stonefish *Synanceia verrucosa*

One of the world's deadliest fish is scarcely more than one foot long. Thirteen venomous spines grow down its back, and a single touch can injure or kill an unlucky human. This hunter is hard to see because its brown or gray color makes it look like a rough rock. Patches of red, orange, and yellow help it blend into coral. Sharks and rays are immune to stonefish poison and prey on them, if they can find them. People can eat them, too, because stonefish venom is harmless after it's cooked.

Learn more!

Parker, Steve. *Ocean and Sea*. New York: Scholastic, 2012.

You can also visit the library or use the Internet to find out more about the specific ocean creatures in this book.

REPTILES & AMPHIBIANS

Gray Tree Frog *Hyla versicolor*

Six gray tree frogs could fit on a twelve-inch ruler. But its small size doesn't stop a tiny male from loudly croaking from treetops to attract a female. The frog's lumpy skin looks warty and helps the frog blend in against tree bark. The tree frog can change color from almost black to nearly white. Its bright yellow leg patches show only when it jumps. So when danger appears, it sits tight!

Copperhead *Agkistrodon contortrix*

A copperhead likes rocky outcroppings and forest floors, where it hunts by hiding in dead leaves. An unwary mouse or vole that creeps too near may never know what hit it. Young copperheads are born rather than hatched from eggs like most snakes. They use their brightly colored tails as bait to attract prey.

Adults sometimes climb trees to hunt. The copperhead is venomous and has a painful bite that needs to be treated immediately.

Young Bullfrog *Lithobates catesbeianus*

A bullfrog's motto might be "Eat it before it eats you." Big bullfrogs eat snakes, fish, birds, turtles, and other frogs. During mating season, males serenade females with deep croaking sounds. Females lay up to twenty thousand eggs at a time, which take three years to grow from tadpoles into adults. A young bullfrog hides among shore weeds, lily pads, or cattails, camouflaged by its green and olive-brown spotted skin. When danger is near, the bullfrog gives a short, high-pitched yelp and leaps into the water for safety.

American Alligator *Alligator mississippiensis*

Spanish explorers called it *el lagarto*, the lizard. Big alligators weigh eight hundred pounds and can reach thirteen feet, twice as long and three times as heavy as a black bear. When one of these giant reptiles swims toward its target, most of its body is hidden, like a leathery iceberg. Alligators are found in ten states, but Louisiana and Florida have the largest populations—more than one million each. In spring a bull (male) bellowing for a cow (female) is an awesome sound.

LEARN MORE!

Winner, Cherie. *Everything Reptile: What Kids Really Want to Know About Reptiles*. Chanhassen, MN: NorthWord Press, 2004.

Taylor-Butler, Christine. *Amphibians*. New York: Children's Press, 2014.

You can also visit the library or use the Internet to find out more about the specific reptiles and amphibians in this book.

Mammals

Bengal Tiger *Panthera tigris tigris*
What cat can weigh more than six hundred pounds, measure ten feet long from nose to tail, swim eighteen miles in a day, dash thirty-five miles per hour, and eat seventy pounds of meat in one meal? A Bengal tiger. A tiger hunts alone, ambushing prey from tall grass or forest shadows that conceal its stripes. It prefers deer, antelope, and pigs, but can kill a water buffalo six times its size. All species of tiger are endangered—there are only three thousand to four thousand left in the wild.

Fawn *Cervidae*
Baby deer are tasty treats for prowling predators. They are too little to run and too weak to defend themselves, so they drop to the ground and curl up. They are odorless, so predators can't smell them, and white spots scattered over their back and sides make it hard to see them in the sunlight and shadows on the forest floor. The mother deer, called a doe, bolts ahead to lead hunters on a wild chase away from her fawn, going back later to lead the fawn to safety.

Eastern Gray Squirrel *Sciurus carolinensis*
Gray squirrels are born hairless, toothless, and blind, but become adults in only one year. A country squirrel may live six years. Townies face more cars, and many don't last even one year. A squirrel prefers seeds, nuts, buds, and fruits, but insects, eggs, and even young snakes will do in a pinch. It's an acrobat and a master of avoiding pursuit. When threatened, it can climb, leap from limb to limb, or dive into a hole. Many a squirrel hunter has gone home empty-handed.

Polar Bear *Ursus maritimus*
The polar bear loves ice. A layer of fat below its hide and fur keeps it cozy in the coldest blizzards. It has many nicknames, but one that fits it well is "Seal's Dread," because its favorite meal is seal blubber. The bear can smell a seal a mile away. It'll sit patiently at the ice's edge for a seal to surface, but if it has to chase one down, it can sprint on great, wide paws at twenty-five miles an hour.

Learn more!
Sill, Cathryn. *About Mammals: A Guide for Children*. Atlanta, GA: Peachtree, 1997.

You can also visit the library or use the Internet to find out more about the specific mammals in this book.

Insects & Spiders

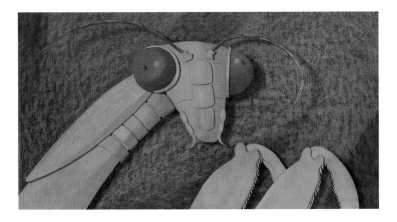

Bumblebee Moth *Hemaris diffinis*

The bumblebee moth is also called the snowberry clearwing, and it has no stinger. It's a defenseless moth that fools birds by looking like a bumblebee. It flies like a bumblebee, hums like a bumblebee, and feeds on the same flowers as bumblebees. Most moths are nocturnal, but the bumblebee moth flies by day to mimic bumblebees. They hide their small, round, green eggs by sticking them to the bottoms of leaves.

Crab Spider *Thomisidae*

There's no web needed for this hungry little eight-legged hunter. Some types gradually turn the same color as the flower they perch on. Others are the color of their habitat. Sooner or later an unsuspecting fly, mosquito, or bee drops by, and dinner is served. Some kinds of crab spiders hunt by prowling into crevices or through grass and leaf litter. These unique spiders hold their front legs up like crab claws and scuttle backward or sideways like crabs on a beach.

Praying Mantis *Mantis religiosa*

Strong young mantises eat their weaker siblings. Bigger ones will eat small birds, snakes, and rodents. Mantises blend in with the background, remain patiently still, and then ambush their prey. A mantis sometimes bites off the head of an insect before devouring it. When threatened, a mantis may stand tall, spread its front legs, fan out its wings, and hiss to scare pursuers. It's good that praying mantises aren't the size of a T. rex!

Walking Stick *Phasmatodea*

Whatever it's called—walking stick, stick insect, stick-bug, ghost insect—it's a master of disguise. There are three thousand types of walking sticks, and all are hard to find. Is that a leaf? A piece of bark? A twig? A walking stick hides well from animals that hunt it. When threatened, a walking stick can give off a smelly secretion that hurts the attacker's mouth and eyes. It might flash its wings or make a loud noise. If all else fails, it throws up a vile vomit to scare off those who want to eat it!

Learn More!

Johnson, Jinny. *Children's Guide to Insects and Spiders*. New York: Simon & Schuster, 1996.

You can also visit the library or use the Internet to find out more about the specific insects and spiders in this book.

Birds

Screech Owl *Megascops*

For such a loudmouth, the screech owl is a pipsqueak measuring less than twelve inches tall. By day it holes up in a tree, invisible against the background. By night it trills a spooky cry and sets to work pouncing on unsuspecting prey. It's not a finicky eater—anything from worms and insects to songbirds, small mammals, and rodents will do. The ground below its roost becomes littered with bits of fur, feathers, and bones.

Great Blue Heron *Ardea herodias*

A great blue heron can stand four feet tall. It flaps along a riverbank or shoreline with a six-foot wingspan. How can such an enormous bird use camouflage to hunt? It stands as still as a statue. Then, edging slowly, it surprises fish, frogs, grasshoppers, mice, and lizards that find themselves within striking distance of its dagger-like bill. During mating season, up to one thousand herons build their nests one hundred feet off the ground in the same cluster of trees. Ten weeks after hatching, young herons are on their own.

Hawk *Accipitriformes*

Hawks come from a big family of meat eaters. Among their cousins are eagles and buzzards. From red-tailed hawks with wingspans of forty-three inches to sparrow hawks half that size, these intelligent birds use sharp eyesight to pick out movement on the ground below. The hawk soars and circles high above trees and open fields, and no mouse, lizard, vole, wood rat, rabbit, or ground squirrel is safe when it hurtles from the sky. Young hawks leave the nest six weeks after hatching and can live for more than twenty years.

Learn More!

Burnie, David. *Bird*. New York: DK Publishers, 2008.

You can also visit the library or use the Internet to find out more about the specific birds in this book.